IØ136931

Washington Gladden

Was Bronson Alcott's School a Type of God's Moral Government?

A Review of Joseph Cook's tTheory of the Atonement

Washington Gladden

Was Bronson Alcott's School a Type of God's Moral Government?
A Review of Joseph Cook's tTheory of the Atonement

ISBN/EAN: 9783744783606

Printed in Europe, USA, Canada, Australia, Japan

Cover: Foto ©Lupo / pixelio.de

More available books at **www.hansebooks.com**

WAS

BRONSON ALCOTT'S SCHOOL

A TYPE OF

GOD'S MORAL GOVERNMENT?

A REVIEW OF

JOSEPH COOK'S THEORY OF THE ATONEMENT.

BY

WASHINGTON GLADDEN.

BOSTON:
LOCKWOOD, BROOKS, AND COMPANY.
1877.

THEORIES OF THE ATONEMENT.

No small stir has been made in religious circles during the last winter, by the lectures of the Rev. Joseph Cook, in the city of Boston, upon various topics of science, philosophy, and religion. Mr. Cook has been hailed as the champion of the orthodox faith long hoped for, come at last; his lectures have been listened to by crowded and applauding congregations, and read in various newspaper reports by a multitude of people.

In one respect, at least, his work has been a remarkable success. To have got, for such themes, so wide a hearing, is in itself a notable feat of intellect. And I, for one, am neither prepared to deny nor disposed to doubt that much of this discussion has been of great service to the highest interests. In Mr. Cook's criticisms of the materialistic philosophy (which is no philosophy) ; in his sharp call for the previous question, which the modern sceptics are determined not to hear; in his exposures of the flimsy logic by which the positions of godless science are often reached, — he has shown the inconclusiveness of much of the current unbelief, and has helped to strengthen the faith of men in the things that are unseen and eternal. I am also indebted to him for clear statements of some truths of theology, and for many stimulating suggestions.

Nevertheless I am not yet convinced that Mr. Cook is infallible; and over some of the roads that are now well beaten by his repetitious assertions my thought refuses to follow him.

Perhaps it is given to few of us to know when we are doing our best work. That with which we are best satisfied is not always our highest achievement. In Mr. Cook's own opinion, his theological masterpiece seems to be his restatement of the doctrine of the atonement; but, to those who look on more coolly from without, this judgment is open to some questioning. It may turn out, after a little space, that his credit as a philosopher has been damaged by his speculations on this subject more than by any thing else that he has undertaken.

I have ventured upon a somewhat careful examination of Mr. Cook's theory of the atonement; and I beg leave to state very briefly my reasons for doing so.

In the first place, the subject has been brought sharply before the public; men are thinking about it everywhere; and, if the truth be not all told, it may be well to tell a little more of it. Mr. Cook has rather rudely brushed away, in his denials, doctrines which many good Christians yet believe; and he has tried to put in their place something which he regards as more rational. His denials have been more effective than his affirmations. He has made it plain that some things that have been believed hitherto can be believed no longer; but he has by no means made it plain what we are to believe in their stead. The work of theological reconstruction is always easy, so far as the pulling-down process is concerned: the rebuilding process is quite another thing. And the structure which Mr. Cook has put in place of those theories of the atonement once held is so badly planned and so poorly built that they who take refuge in it are sure before long to find it tumbling down upon their heads. It is the simple duty of those by whom the defects of this theory are clearly seen, to point them out to those who have not seen them.

In the second place, a thorough examination of the doctrine of the atonement ought to be, in itself, a useful exercise. The theme is one that is worthy of our most reverent and most ener-

getic thought; and, although the conclusion of
our deepest investigations will leave many
things connected with it in mystery, yet we
may hope to reach some explanation of the
work of Christ that shall accord with our reason, and that shall not conflict with the spirit of
God's word.

It ought to be said, however, at the outset,
that the belief of no given theory of the
atonement is essential to the salvation of any
individual. Men are not saved by believing
theories of the atonement: they are saved by
believing on Christ.

Two physicians may agree as to the medicine
that ought to be prescribed for a sick man, and
yet have very different theories as to how the
medicine works. Experience may have proved
to both of them that it is the right medicine to
give, because it always cures the disease; but,
when they undertake to explain the philosophy
of the cure, they may greatly differ. It is *important* that they should understand (and it may
be well enough that the patient should himself
understand) just how the medicine works; but
it is not *essential* to the cure of this patient, that
the doctors or the patient should know all the
process by which the cure is effected: the *essential* thing is, that the doctors should give the
medicine, and that the patient should take it.

Just so the remedy for sin is trust in Jesus Christ, acceptance of him as Saviour and Lord. It is well that the teacher of religion and the Christian believer should have some consistent explanation of the way in which Christ saves us, but it is not essential that we know *how* he does it: the essential thing is that we should let him do it. Of course we must have some clear belief about Christ himself, that he is One who is able to save to the uttermost all that come to him, or we shall not intrust ourselves to him. But if we have a confidence in his power and willingness to save us which leads us to accept him as our Saviour, and to devote our lives to his service, we may be saved by him from sin, even though our philosophy of salvation may be altogether imperfect.

A little study of the history of doctrines will make it evident that belief in a theory of the atonement is not essential to salvation. For the first thousand years after Christ, the great majority of the theologians taught that Christ was a ransom delivered by God to the devil for the deliverance of the human race. The theory was by no means uniform in its statement, but in the general representation the atonement was made to be either a bargain or a contest between God and the devil, in which, either by force or by fraud on the part of God, or by blundering or over-reaching on the part of the devil, the legal rights of the latter in the human race were extinguished. Dr. Dale speaks none too strongly when he characterizes this theory of ransom as not only " rude and coarse," but also as intolerable, " monstrous, and profane."

Anselm's theory came next; and, in a moral point of view, it was a great improvement on that which it superseded. This theory represents the work of Christ as restoring to God the honor of which sin had robbed him ; as paying the debt due to God on account of sin. As he was man, perfect obedience was required of him : that he rendered. But the suffering of death could not have been required of him : when as the God-man he endured that, he did just so much more than he was under obligation to do, and accumulated a fund of surplus merit, out of which the debts of all who believe on him are paid.

Then followed the theory of the reformers, Luther, Calvin, and their contemporaries, in which the doctrine that Christ is our legal substitute, and that the penalty of our sins is inflicted upon him, obtains its first clear and emphatic statement.

After this came the governmental theory of the great publicist, Grotius, elaborated in later years by the New-England theologians, and forming the basis of Mr. Cook's doctrine, which we are presently to examine.

All of these theories, it will be observed, are or have been "orthodox." Now, if salvation depends on the belief of any given theory, the great majority of professing Christians must have been lost, for not one of these has been believed by any thing more than a fraction of the Church; and they are by no means the same in substance; they are utterly unlike: they are even contradictory. And the thought easily suggests itself, that a doctrine which has passed through so many changes of form may even yet be subject to modifications; that quite possibly it has not received its final statements even in the glowing orations of Joseph Cook.

Let us proceed now to examine his theory, as set forth in the lecture delivered at the Tremont Temple, April 16, 1877. The authorized report of this lecture contains considerable matter that was not delivered on that day: it is, we may therefore conclude, not an unpremeditated utterance, but a carefully elaborated statement of the doctrine. The lecture of April 23 extends the discussion, but I do not see that it adds any thing to the positions taken in the previous discourse. I wish to do Mr. Cook no injustice, and I shall therefore reproduce *seriatim* every one of his twenty-seven propositions, giving due heed to the arguments and illustrations by which he seeks to establish them.

"1. It is self-evident that a thing cannot be and not be at the same time and in the same sense."   ·

Beyond doubt this is true. Mr. Cook's starting-point is a long way off from his goal, and he takes a good many steps that he might have saved himself and the rest of us.

"2. It is therefore self-evident, that we cannot be at once at peace and at variance with conscience;
"3. That we cannot be at once at peace and at variance with the record of our past;
"4. That we cannot be at once at peace and at variance with God."

To all these deductions from the initial axiom we shall, no doubt, give our immediate assent.

"5. It is self-evident, that, while we continue to exist as personalities of the same plan we now exhibit in our natures, conscience will be something we cannot escape from."

If this means that we shall always know that there is a difference between right and wrong, and that we shall always feel that we ought to do the right and shun the wrong, I agree to it. If it means that our moral judgments concerning our actions are always the same, I deny it.

Conscience may, in the past, have pronounced certain actions wrong that it now pronounces right. The man who has been converted to Protestantism from the Roman Catholic faith once thought it wrong to read the Protestant Bible, or to receive the sacrament from the hands of a Protestant minister. What he once thought wrong he now thinks right. We may not escape from conscience, but we may escape from many of the restraints and many of the obligations that conscience has laid upon us.

" 6. It is self-evident that our past is irreversible."

Yea, verily! Hold fast to this truth, for it will be needed to steady us in our argument when we get a little further on. Mr. Cook speaks truly and wisely when he affirms that " forever and forever the losses occasioned by what ought not to have been will continue," and that " there will be regret in the universe forever and forever on account of the losses sin has occasioned ; " that " some part of that shadow will fall on the sea of glass, and will not be invisible from the great white throne." Nothing that man can do, nothing that God can do, can annihilate a fact, or make that to be right which once was wrong. The wrong thing that you have done cannot be undone, and it cannot by any power human or divine be made to be a right thing.

"7. It is self-evident that we cannot escape from our record."

By our record I suppose that the lecturer must mean our memory of the past. Concerning this I should not say that it is "self-evident" that we cannot permanently forget what has been. Still I think it is, on the whole, improbable that we should entirely forget any thing that we have known: the facts of mental science indicate the permanence of memory, and make it seem likely that what has temporarily slipped from our recollection may and will return to us again ; but this belief rests on probable evidence, and it is grossly inaccurate to say that the thing is " self-evident."

" 8 [It is self-evident] that we cannot escape from God."

This is evident to Mr. Cook, doubtless, as it is to me ; but the scientific accuracy of the statement that it is *self*-evident may be questioned. Surely it cannot be if we accept Webster's definition of that term. " A self-evident truth," he says, is a truth that is evident without proof or reasoning ; that produces certainty or clear conviction upon a bare presentation to the mind.

That two and three make five, is self-evident.
Now, the fact that we cannot escape from God
involves the fact of God's existence; and the
belief in the existence of God is an inference
rather than an intuition. I heard one of the
students at Andover, the other day, recite twenty-six elaborate propositions set forth by Prof.
Park merely as *preliminary* to the proof of the
existence of God. I do not think that Prof.
Park is a man who would use twenty-six propositions in *getting ready* to show that a thing is
true which was " self-evident " before he began.

" 9. [It is self-evident] that harmonization with our
environment is the indispensable condition of peace of soul;

" 10. That our environment in this world and the next
consists unalterably of God, conscience, and our record."

I do not quite understand Mr. Cook when
he makes conscience part of our environment.
Conscience is either the voice of God within
the soul, or a constituent part of the soul itself.
If it is the voice of God, then Mr. Cook's statement is tautological: if it is part of the soul
itself, then it is no part of the soul's environment: you might as well say that the stamen
of a plant is part of the plant's environment.
What Mr. Cook is laboring to say when he
makes use of these rather pedantic expressions is simply this: that no man can be at

peace in his soul who remembers unforgiven sin against God. And that is probably true, though as we shall see by and by it is a truth that needs to be spoken with some qualifications. There may be such a peace as the peace of death, into which the sinner may fall.

The next three propositions are scarcely new, but they are true beyond question.

"11. [It is self-evident] that we must be free from the love of what ought not to be, before we can be at peace with the moral law which requires what ought to be.

"12. It is self-evident that conscience produces in us a sense of ill-desert whenever we say 'I will not,' to the divine 'I ought.'

"13. That conscience produces in us this sense of ill-desert whenever we accurately remember the record of our intelligent refusal to say 'I will,' to the divine 'I ought.'"

Mr. Cook's fourteenth proposition I should have been inclined to accept; but, as I read his own exposition of it, I was not quite clear that he had not succeeded in disproving the thing that he was trying to prove.

"14. That no lapse of time lessens this sense of ill-desert [occasioned by the remembrance of our refusal to obey the moral law] if the memory of such refusal is vivid and thoughtful."

In enforcing this proposition, Mr. Cook recalls

the assassination of President Lincoln, and asks whether the lapse of time has changed *our* opinion " as to the blameworthiness of the principal actor in it." Perhaps not; but whether it has or no is neither here nor there, so far as his proposition is concerned : the only question is whether Wilkes Booth's opinion of the transaction has changed. The question concerning *our* opinions is wholly irrelevant. The illustration does not illustrate.

The next case supposed by Mr. Cook comes nearer to his proposition. " It is a terrible certainty that Judas Iscariot, if he ever blamed himself once justly, must continue to blame himself forever and forever." Well, that, at any rate, is the thing to be proved. " There is a noose," he proceeds to say, " that a man may put about his neck, and tie, which he cannot untie. There is irreversibility in the past, and the action which ought not to have been will always be regarded as such when we vividly and faithfully remember its character. . . . Conscience is so fearfully and wonderfully made, that you must forever disapprove what ought not to have been." All this is strongly on the side of his proposition. But how about this which immediately follows?

" How evident it is that, under natural law, a man may drift on in careless æsthetic ways till he loses the perception of the beautiful! He learns to love that which æsthetically ought not to be ; and he blunts his æsthetic sense until you say he could, by a long process of culture, be brought back perhaps, but never will be. You say his probation is over æsthetically. On every conceivable side, except the moral and religious, character is subject to probations, and attains permanence. But on these sides a whim of the luxurious ages forbids you to hear the truth which all great and strenuous ages have asserted ; namely, that probations of course exist there, as they do elsewhere. Undeniably there are æsthetical probations, physical probations, and intellectual probations. But now you affirm, you who assert the unity of law, that there are no moral probations. Do you perceive any self-contradiction in that intellectual proceeding ? "

Here in the authorized report of Mr. Cook's lecture I find that there was " profound sensation " in his audience, and I partly believe it ; for it would seem that any good-natured and sympathetic audience must have felt a sensation not only profound, but also rather painful, as it gradually became evident — not to say self-evident — that Mr. Cook was in much the same predicament with Father Taylor when his nominative and his verb got hopelessly parted, and when the good old gentleman suddenly became certain of nothing but that he was bound for the kingdom of heaven.

Mr. Cook's proposition is, if he will suffer us to recall it, that no lapse of time lessens our sense of ill-desert on account of clearly remembered transgressions. His argument is, that the æsthetic nature of men becomes blunted by neglect or misuse of it, until they lose their perception of the beautiful; until they learn to admire that which is not admirable, to think that beautiful which is not beautiful; until they become fixed in this habit of thinking; that, just as there are æsthetical probations, there are moral probations: in other words, as a man may, by abusing his æsthetic nature, come to think a thing beautiful which once he thought ugly, so a man may, by abusing his moral nature, come to think a thing right which once he thought wrong.

Now, this may be true, or may not; but if it is true the proposition which it is intended to illustrate is not true. The argument exactly contradicts the statement; and if we are to accept Mr. Cook's initial postulate, that a thing cannot be and not be at the same time and in the same sense, we shall be obliged to extinguish either the proposition or its proof.

My own opinion is that the proof is all right,

— the last part of it, I mean, — and that the thing to be proved is all wrong. I believe it to be true, that the moral nature of man is blunted by continuance in sin; that the pain of remembered transgression is lessened as time goes on; that our perceptions of right and wrong are dimmed, and that our power to do the right and shun the wrong is lost, by continuance in sin. A deep truth is here, to which we shall give more attention by and by.

Mr. Cook's next proposition brings us face to face with one of the fundamental questions of theology.

" 15. It is self-evident, on examination of our experience, that conscience, when we keep our eyes open to light, produces in us, besides the sense of ill-desert, a feeling that something ought to be done to satisfy the rightly resplendent majesty, and the plainly unconditional and eternal authority, of the violated law which says, ' I ought.' "

The principal ideas contained in this proposition are these: 1. There is a law (adjectives do not add to its force) which says, " I ought." That is undeniable. 2. When we refuse to obey that law, conscience produces in us a sense of ill-desert. That, too, is beyond question. 3. When we violate that law, conscience produces in us a feeling that something ought to be done to satisfy it. Let us see about this.

The law under consideration is the law that says, "I ought." It is "the law of the mind," of which Paul speaks more than once, — the sense of moral obligation that all men feel, and that constrains them to say not only "I ought," according to Mr. Cook, but a little more than this, — "I ought to do right." Now, when a man has done what he believes to be wrong, his conscience, which is simply the voice within him that utters and enforces the law, "I ought to do right," does produce within him a feeling of ill-desert. But does conscience say that something ought to be done to satisfy this law? How satisfy it? The law within me says, "I ought to do right," and I have done wrong. The past is irreversible; the law is unchangeable. How, then, is it possible that the law should be satisfied? The bad deed cannot be changed to make it agree with the good law; the good law cannot be altered to make it approve the bad deed: between the righteous law and the unrighteous act there is and always will be disagreement. The law would have been satisfied by obedience, but it can be satisfied with nothing short of obedience; by every act of disobedience one of those losses is suffered, which, in Mr. Cook's own words, must continue forever and forever.

I object therefore to the statement that conscience demands "satisfaction" for past disobedience of the law which says, "I ought to do right." Conscience is not irrational; it demands nothing which is absolutely impossible; and it is absolutely impossible that past disobedience should be changed to obedience.

But it will be answered, that what conscience produces in us is feeling that we ought to be punished for past disobedience. The law is satisfied, it will be said, when its penalty is suffered. No: you cannot satisfy, in that way, the law that says, "I ought to do right." No amount of suffering that could be inflicted or endured would be a full equivalent for disobedience. Is it all the same thing, as before that law, whether I do right, or suffer for doing wrong? Is the law equally satisfied with the obedience of those who obey, and the punishment of those who disobey?

Take this question out of the realm of abstractions. The law of which we are talking is the law of God. "I ought to do right," is simply the response of the human nature to the voice out of heaven which says, "Thou oughtest to do right." And is God satisfied when men suffer the penalty of this violated law? Is it all one to him, whether men do right, or whether they refuse to do right and take the consequences? Leaving out of the account, if you

can, his infinite compassion, is his ethical nature
— the principle of righteousness in him —
equally satisfied with the obedience of the good
and the suffering of the evil? These questions
are answered by asking them. We know, if we
know any thing of God, that no equivalents of
suffering will ever compensate him for the sins
of his creatures.

Let us be done, therefore, with talking about
satisfying the law of righteousness. In a loose
popular sense, it may be said that human laws
are "satisfied" when the penalty annexed to
them is inflicted. All that is meant by that
phrase is that the state has reached the limit
which it has assigned to itself in punishing the
offence. But this analogy does not at all help
us in comprehending the obligations of men to
the law that is spiritual, — the eternal law of
right. That law is not of such a nature that it
can be satisfied in this way. That law, when it
has once been disobeyed, cannot be satisfied by
man nor by God, neither in this life nor in the
life to come. That is "the shadow that will
rest on the sea of glass for ever and ever."

But it will be said that conscience does produce in us the feeling that punishment is deserved, and ought to be inflicted. That is true;
but the feeling that I deserve punishment is
very different from the feeling that something

must be done to satisfy the law. It is not a governmental feeling : it is a personal feeling. The criminal whose moral nature is not wholly perverted feels instinctively that *he* is to blame, and that *he* ought to be punished. If his conscience forces him, as conscience sometimes does, to come and give himself up to the officers of the law, it is not because he feels that the law ought to be vindicated: it is because he feels that he, an evil-doer, ought to suffer for his crime. The political philosopher who hears of the occurrence, and the judge who administers the sentence, may argue that the criminal ought to be punished for the protection of the state ; but that is not the instinctive feeling of the criminal himself. He does not think of the honor that is due to the government, but of the retribution that is due to him as a malefactor.

And this is precisely the feeling that arises in the human soul, on the remembrance of every violation of the moral law. The transgressor feels that he has done wrong, and that he ought to be punished.

"16. It is self-evident on examination of personal and general experience, that in the absence of satisfaction [and satisfaction is always absent] conscience forebodes punishment."

"It is self-evident, on examination of personal and general experience." What sort of "science" is this? Nothing can be *self*-evident, that is only evident on examination of " personal and general experience," that a man does not know until he has read history. It is like Mr. John Phœnix's saying that the autograph of a certain man was undoubtedly genuine, as it was written by one of his most intimate friends. The autograph of the intuition is not written by " personal and general experience." I dwell upon this because it is a vice of Mr. Cook's method. He wants to make it appear that this argument of his is in the nature of a mathematical demonstration, and therefore he calls many things axioms which are not axioms at all. Such a misuse of language vitiates a great part of his reasoning.

All that can be saved from the wreck of this proposition is the last three words, " conscience forebodes punishment." I know that this is true so far as I am concerned; and, while nothing that takes place in other men's minds can be " self-evident" to me, I have no doubt that it is true of other men.

The next five propositions need not detain us long.

"17. That it [conscience] forebodes this [punishment] with such force and pertinacity that this action of con-

science, according to the confession of all great literature
and philosophy, makes cowards of us all.

"18. That it forebodes punishment not only in this life,
but in time to come beyond death.

"19. This foreboding has done as much work in the
history of religion as any other instinct, and thus has
proved its strength."

To all these statements no word of dissent
need be interposed. The meaning of this instinctive expectation of punishment in this life
and in the life beyond will be plainer to us by
and by; but the fact is one that no sound philosophy will attempt to deny.

"20. Foreboding does not cease when we become free
from the love of sin.

"21. It is self-evident, therefore, that the absence of the
love of sin in the present does not bring us to peace when
we vividly and thoughtfully recall our record of sin in the
past, and allow our native instincts free course."

To these statements objection will be made.
"Why," it will be asked, "should the fear of
punishment continue when we have ceased from
sinning?" Whether it should continue or not,
it does: that is certain. And we can see some
reasons why it does; for the fact that we are
doing right in the present does not alter the fact
that we did wrong in the past, does not change
the fact of our blameworthiness for that wrong-

doing, does not obliterate our knowledge of the fact that we deserve punishment for that wrong-doing. Mr. Cook is quite right about this. It is a shallow philosophy which supposes that present obedience makes amends for past disobedience, or silences the voice of conscience that tells of past guilt and forebodes punishment. If that voice is ever to be quieted, it must be done by something else besides our own efforts at reformation. How, then, is it done? Let us hear Mr. Cook tell us truly, in the first place, how it is not done.

" 22. It is self-evident that personal ill-desert cannot be removed from person to person."

That is a sound proposition, and here is the argument by which it is supported : —

" What! sin not taken off us, and put upon our Lord? Our guilt not borne by our Saviour? No : not in the sense in which you understand guilt. Blameworthiness is not transferred from us to him, and cannot be. We know that our Lord had no sin, and that there can be no taking off personal ill-desert from one personality, and putting it upon another. . . . Our Lord is no murderer, no perjurer. There is no divergence of theological opinion from self-evident truth, when self-evident truth declares that personal

demerit is not transferable from personality to
personality. . . . We have no doctrine of the
atonement which declares that personal demerit
is laid upon our Lord, or that, in the strict sense
of the word, he suffered punishment, that is,
pain inflicted for personal blameworthiness.
He was an innocent being, as he always will be,
and never did, can, or will suffer punishment in
the strict sense of that word."

That is a fair representation of one phase of
orthodoxy; but Mr. Cook is not justified in
leaving it to be inferred that orthodoxy has no
other phase.   When he says, as he does elsewhere, that " evangelical scholarship abhors "
the idea " that God punishes by substitution,"
and the idea " that Christ, though innocent,
was punished," he is very far from telling the
whole truth.   Dr. Charles Hodge of Princeton
says that Christ saves his people " by bearing
the penalty of the law in their stead."   That
' Christ's sufferings were penal, were *judicially*
inflicted in satisfaction of justice ; " that " he
suffered the penalty of the law ; " that " his
sufferings were neither calamities, nor chastise-
ments designed for his own benefit, nor merely
dogmatic or symbolical or exemplary," — Dr.
Hodge distinctly teaches.[1]   His son Prof. A. A.
Hodge, of Allegheny, who has just been called

---

[1] Hodge's Theology, vol. ii. p. 474.

to succeed his father at Princeton, is even more explicit. He affirms that Christ did suffer "the very penalty of the law, because he suffered in our stead; our sins were punished in strict rigor of justice in him." Mr. Cook says, as we shall presently see, that the sufferings of Christ were not a penalty, but the substitute for a penalty. Prof. Hodge says that this phrase is absurd: "sin is either punished, or it is not punished," he says; there is no such thing as a substitute for punishment. These men are not alone, as Mr. Cook ought to know. The dogma that they teach is the very dogma of the Presbyterian standards; and there are few if any Presbyterian or Dutch Reformed theological seminaries in the country where it is not diligently taught. Mr. Cook denounces the Liberals of Boston for representing "evangelical scholarship" as teaching that "God punishes by substitution," and that "Christ, an innocent being, was punished;" and his audience receives his denunciation with "great applause"! "The scientific method" would seem to have been slightly strained in this proceeding.

Let us, however, admit that this statement of his concerning the sufferings of Christ is true, as far as it goes, even though all "evangelical scholarship" should deny it. "Christ never did, can, or will suffer punishment in the strict sense of that word." " Personal ill-desert cannot be removed from person to person." That, at any rate, ought to be self-evident. I know, if I know any thing, that my sins cannot be imputed or charged over to another person, or assumed by another person ; that no other person can be considered *guilty* on account of what I have done, or be *punished* in my stead. But now Mr. Cook makes a distinction which brings his theory of the atonement before us : " That word ' guilt' is a fog, unless you remember that behind it lie two meanings. Guilt signifies, first, personal blameworthiness ; second, obligation to render satisfaction to violated law. In the former sense, guilt cannot be transferred from person to person ; in the latter, it can be." And thus we come to the propositions in which the doctrine, as he understands it, is set forth.

" 23. Guilt in the second sense, or obligation to satisfy the demands of a violated law, may be removed when the Author of the law substitutes his own voluntary sacrificial chastisement for our punishment.

" 24. When such a substitution is made, the highest possible motives to loyalty to that Ruler are brought to bear upon the rebellious subject.

" 25. If any great arrangement on this principle has been made by the Father, Redeemer, and Sanctifier of the universe, that arrangement meets with exactness the deepest wants of man. It is the highest possible dissuasive from the love of sin ; it is the only possible deliverance from the guilt of sin, in the sense, not of personal blameworthiness, but of obligation to satisfy the violated law which says, ' I ought.'

" 26. Such a great arrangement may therefore, with scientific exactness, be known to be needed, and so needed as to be called properly the desire of all nations.

" 27. The atonement which reason can prove is needed, revelation declares has been made."

These are the concluding propositions of Mr. Cook's analysis. Let us see now what are the principles on which his theory rests. The key of the whole position is in these sentences : " Guilt in the sense of blameworthiness cannot be transferred from person to person : guilt in the sense of obligation to satisfy the demands of violated law *can* be transferred from person to person."

Now, in the face of all this, I affirm that guilt in neither of these senses can be transferred. I say that you can no more transfer punishableness than you can transfer blameworthiness ; that, if there be any such thing as obligation to satisfy the law which says, " I ought," that obligation must rest on him who has violated the law, and can no more be transferred to anybody else than down can be up, or than wrong can be right. The absolute personality of moral obligation in every phase of it ; the absolute impossibility of shirking it, or being relieved of it, or transferring it ; the absolute

certainty that no " arrangement " has been
made, or can be made, in heaven or on earth,
whereby any part of my moral obligation can
be transferred to or assumed by any other
being, human or divine, — I take to be the very
foundation-stones of ethical science. Others
may suffer on account of my sins ; others may
voluntarily take upon themselves suffering in
seeking to save me from my sins ; in this man-
ner Christ does suffer for me : but to affirm
that any part of my obligation to satisfy the
law which says, " I ought," can be transferred
to any other being, is to contradict one of the
first principles of morality.

How, pray, can the law which says, " I
ought," be satisfied ? Only by obedience, as
we have seen. Past disobedience cannot be
changed into obedience by any transfer. The
past is irreversible. The law within me says,
" I ought to do right ; " and I have done wrong.
That fact cannot be altered. But there is
something more. The feeling within me says,
" I ought to be punished for my wrong-doing."
My feeling is not that *somebody* ought to suffer,
but that *I* ought to suffer. That is a natural
and a just feeling. But the instinct which
says, " I ought to suffer," cannot be satisfied
with inflicting suffering on somebody else.

I feel that I ought to suffer if I have violated

the law which says, " I ought to do right;" but
my suffering by no means satisfies the law.
How, then, can it be satisfied, or how can peace
be restored to my soul, by the suffering of one
who ought *not* to suffer ?

The principles here enunciated cannot be
proved. They can only be stated. To my mind
they are axioms. It seems to me that they
ought to be axioms to every person who has a
conscience. I cannot doubt that to every good
man they will be plain some day, — in the next
world if not in this.

Mr. Cook says that obligation to satisfy the
demands of a violated law may be removed by
the author of the law. But who is the author
of the law that says, " I ought to do right" ?
Do you say that it is God ? Stop and think.
Is not that law eternal ? Is it not the very
condition of moral existence ? Is not God himself under obligation to that law, just as really
as you and I are under obligation to it ? Is
what he does right because he does it, or does
he do what he does because it is right ? There
are some things that God cannot do. He
cannot make two and two five, and he cannot remove from any being in the universe a
particle of the obligation that the law of right
imposes. I do not mean that there is any
power above God to enforce this law upon him,

but rather that the ideal law of right rules his thought so perfectly that he could not set it aside without denying himself.

You say that God is just: does not that imply that there is an ideal law of justice with which you compare his judgments? You say that God's acts are right: does not that mean that there is an ideal law of right to which his conduct conforms?

Well, then, we may take issue with Mr. Cook right here, and reverently deny that God can remove any obligation that the eternal law of right imposes. That is only another way of saying that God can neither do nor sanction wrong. God is not in any such sense the author of the eternal law of right (and this is the only law, let it be observed, of which Mr. Cook has spoken), that he can remove any portion of the obligations of that law.

But Mr. Cook says that God has done this very thing. How? By "substituting his own voluntary sacrificial chastisement for our punishment." No, that cannot be: the chastisement of an innocent being, whether divine or human, cannot be substituted for the punishment of a guilty one. That is not just; that is not right; and therefore, because God is both just and righteous, he will do nothing of the kind. It is contrary to the nature of things; it is contrary to the nature of God ; and therefore it cannot be.

Nevertheless Mr. Cook thinks that he has found, in a transaction that occurred some years ago in Boston, an analogy that shows how the punishment of one may be removed by substituting for it the voluntary sacrificial chastisement of another. I do him no injustice when I say that this illustration is the corner-stone of his system. He has repeated it twice in Boston within a few weeks, and he most strenuously asserts that it contains the principle of the atonement. Let us have the illustration in Mr. Cook's own words : —

" On the slope of Beacon Hill a New-England author, who ought always to be named side by side with Pestalozzi, once made it a rule that if a pupil violated its (*sic*) regulations the master should substitute his own voluntary sacrificial chastisement for that pupil's punishment."

We may perhaps be permitted to doubt whether this was the exact language of the rule. Mr. Alcott sometimes uses large words, but it is not likely that he ever said any thing to his pupils about "substituting his own voluntary sacrificial chastisement for their punishment." What he said was, I presume, something like this : " Boys, if you whisper, I shall not whip you, but I shall make you whip me."

"Bronson Alcott will allow me to say here and now in his presence, that he has told me that this one regulation almost Christianized his school. The pupils were quite young, and for that reason the measure was effective among them. He was no dreamer: he would never have adopted this measure except with the sensitive. Nevertheless the operation of these untutored, hardly unfolded, and therefore unstained hearts, indicated what man is. 'One day,' says Bronson Alcott, 'I called up before me a pupil eight or ten years of age, who had violated an important regulation of the school. All the pupils were looking on, and they knew what the rule of the school was. I put the ruler into the hand of that offending pupil; I extended my hand; I told him to strike. The instant the boy saw my extended hand, and heard my command to strike, I saw a struggle begin in his face. A new light sprang up in his countenance; a new set of shuttles seemed to be weaving a new nature within him. I kept my hand extended, and the school was in tears. I constantly watched his face, and he seemed in a bath of fire which was giving him a new nature. He had a different mood toward the school and toward the violated law. The boy seemed transformed by the idea that I should take chastisement in place of his punishment.

He went back to his seat, and ever after was one of the most docile of all the pupils in that school, although he had been at first one of the rudest.'"

That is the story. Now for Mr. Cook's application of it. After a somewhat eloquent commentary upon the transaction, he proceeds, as he says, to "summarize the truths contained in this discussion, by asserting, in the name of the axioms of the nature of things, that it is clear : —

" 1. That the master of that school was not guilty."

No, he was not. Go on.

" 2. That he suffered, in the strict sense, not punishment, but chastisement."

He suffered neither ; but let us wait and see.

" 3. That he had power to remove from the pupil the obligation to satisfy the law of the school."

What was the law of the school? For substance, I suppose it must have been, " Do right." What the particular regulations may have been, I do not know ; but if the command to do right was not the substance of them, they were not binding upon the pupils, and the obligation " to satisfy them " could not be removed, because there could not have been any such obligation. If the command to do right *was* the substance

of them, then the obligation " to satisfy them "
could not have been removed by Mr. Alcott nor
any one else.   But of course Mr. Cook means
that the teacher had the power to remove from
the pupil the punishment that was due to him.
Power he might have had : whether he had the
right to remove it, is not so clear.   But we will
not dispute about that.   Grant that he had the
power to remove the punishment : did he remove
it? *Most certainly he did not ; but inflicted it,
vigorously, mercilessly, thoroughly, upon the pupil.*

What was the punishment threatened against
every violator of the law of this school? *It
was that he should whip the master.* To the
pupils the master said, " If you break these
laws, I shall punish you by compelling you to
chastise me."   Mr. Cook says that these were
young, delicately-nurtured, sensitive children.
He gives us Mr. Alcott's word that no such
measure would have been tried with children
who were not peculiarly sensitive.   He knew
that he could punish them more effectually by
making them chastise him, than by inflicting
physical suffering upon them.   He knew that
their sensibilities were more easily hurt than
the palms of their hands ; that they would
rather be whipped themselves than to whip
their teacher.   And therefore his punishment
was so contrived as to strike them in the tender-

est part of their nature, and thus to act as the
strongest possible dissuasive from transgression.
Many of us know children on whom such a
method of discipline would work in just this
way; and some of us know children on whom
it would not work at all. But, beyond a doubt,
this was the reason of the measure; and, if we
may believe the story, its wisdom was in this
case justified.

Let us hear the rest of Mr. Cook's exposition: —

" 4. That after hé [Alcott] had substituted
voluntary sacrificial chastisement on the part
of the master for the punishment due to the
pupil, you cannot demand a second time punishment from that pupil."

But there was no substitution. The law of
the school was enforced; the penalty threatened against the transgressor was literally and
exactly visited upon him: he was made to
strike his master, and, as his master expected,
it hurt him so badly to do it that he took care
never to be made to do it again. That was the
punishment due him; and the reason why he
could not be punished again was, not that something had been substituted for his punishment,
but simply that the punishment had been inflicted. The amazing confusion with which
this argument is covered can only arise from

that coarse materialistic conception of punishment which identifies it with physical suffering; with the sting of a ferule in the open palm, or the torturing flames of a lake of fire and brimstone. Mr. Cook goes on to say, —

" 5. That the pupil's peace before the law of the school is the result not of his own work, but of the master's work; and not of the master's moral influence and general character merely, but of his substitution of chastisement for punishment."

This proposition is repeated in different phraseology once or twice more, but it is hardly worth while to follow the analysis further. " The pupil's peace before the law of the school," so far as this transgression was concerned, resulted from the fact that he had suffered its penalty; his subsequent peace was the result of his obedience.

Mr. Cook says that " in the arc of this little example are involved principles that sweep the whole curve of the atonement," because " law is the same everywhere." " I have a perfect right," he says (in explaining the work of Christ), " to stand on this example of Bronson Alcott's school."

Well, if this transaction gives us the principle of the atonement, we can say nothing but this: that the penalties of God's law are inflicted, to the very letter, upon all transgressors, and that there is no such thing as legal or forensic substitution. Surely there was none here.

Let us draw out now clearly the points of correspondence between this illustration, and the doctrine that it is intended to illustrate.

The penalty of the law of Bronson Alcott's school was thus declared : "If any boy disobey, he shall be compelled to flog the master."

The penalty of the law of God's government is thus declared: "The soul that sinneth, IT shall die. The righteousness of the righteous shall be upon *him*, and the wickedness of the wicked shall be upon HIM," — not in any wise upon his Maker.

In Bronson Alcott's school, the penalty of the law was rigorously inflicted upon the transgressor.

In God's government, as Mr. Cook tells us, the penalty of the law is removed from the transgressor, and "the voluntary sacrificial chastisement" of the ruler is substituted for it.

The two cases, instead of being parallel, are, as anybody can see, exactly at right angles.

I do not care to follow Mr. Cook any further. He has several lectures on this subject that I have not examined here, but I do not see that they add any thing to his argument. I think I have made it plain that his main propositions

contradict the first principles of morality, and
that the example in which, as he says, the principle of the atonement is contained, is openly at
war with his theory.

To show that Mr. Cook's philosophy is inade-
quate, is one thing : to substitute for it an
explanation of the work of Christ, which shall
consist with reason and with conscience, is quite
another thing.   But no critic has a right to
destroy without trying to rebuild.

Some things must be assumed, to begin with.
In the outline of a theory here submitted, it is
assumed that there is one God, that Jesus
Christ is God, and that our moral intuitions are
to be trusted.   I do not say that these postu-
lates are axioms ; but this argument treats them
as truths accepted by those to whom it is ad-
dressed.

The first question we encounter is, *What is
God's moral law?*

In its simplest statement it is the command
to do right.   To this command the conscience
responds, "I ought to do right."   But this command needs to be explained, and Christ has perfectly explained it.   To do right is *to love God
with all the heart, and our neighbors as ourselves.*

The result of obedience to this law is life.
" This do, and thou shalt live," the Saviour said.

But what kind of life is meant? physical life, or spiritual life? Plainly, spiritual life. The body lives by obedience to physical law: the spirit lives by obedience to spiritual law.

The continuance of the life of every thing that lives is the result of obedience to the law of its existence. The law of plant-life requires that light, warmth, moisture, and certain chemical elements be supplied to the plant. If that law is obeyed, the life of the plant is continued. The law of man's spiritual nature requires that it be nourished by loving God with all the heart, and by loving our neighbors as ourselves. While that law is obeyed, spiritual life continues. This is not an arbitrary, but a natural result. God does not make a bargain with the plant, saying, "If you will secure for yourself light and warmth and moisture and the chemical elements that you need, I will continue your existence:" the continuance of the plant's existence is the *natural result* of the supply to the plant of the conditions of its life. Neither does God make a bargain with man, saying, "If you will love me with all the heart, and your neighbor as yourself, I will give to you spiritual life." The spiritual life is the *natural result* of obedience to the soul's law. It is not the price of a commercial arrangement, or the reward of a judicial decree: it is the result of the working of natural laws. The soul has a nature, as well as the plant, and that nature has its laws; and the result of obedience to those laws is life in the soul, as well as in the plant.

They who love God with all the heart are brought into such relations with him that his life is imparted to them, and the principles, motives, judgments, affections, that hold sway in the divine nature, are incorporated into the human nature. By sympathetic communion with any exalted human spirit, we are made partakers, to some degree, of the qualities which belong to that spirit. What is true of our fellowship with men is true in a far higher sense of our fellowship with God. To the fact of this mystic union between God and man, the writers of both Testaments bear abundant witness. It is hardly worth while to multiply proof-texts. The whole Gospel of John might almost be called a monograph on this transcendent theme. The soul that obeys the law of its own nature is thus united with God, and lives by union with him, even as the branch lives by its union with the vine. And the spiritual life that the soul receives by its union with God is eternal life. Since it lives in God, it will live while God lives. It will be a " partaker of the divine nature; " and therefore holiness, health, and peace will be

its eternal portion. Thus it appears that eternal
life is not the commercial equivalent nor the
judicial reward of obedience to the law of the
soul, but the natural and inevitable result of
obedience under the divine constitution.

But what is the consequence of disobedience
to this law ? The answer immediately suggests
itself. If life be the fruit of obedience, death
must be the fruit of disobedience. Such is the
announcement of Scripture, " *The soul that sinneth, it shall die.*"

But death, too, is a word of many significa-
tions. What does it signify in this connection ?
Is it physical death that is annexed to the law
as its penalty ?

Physical death is the consequence of the
violation of physical, not spiritual laws. It is
true that the body and the spirit are so closely
related, that the vigor of the body is promoted
by the peace of the spirit. It is true that, when
the health of the spirit is impaired, the body
always suffers with it. But this is only a sec-
ondary and indirect result. I do not suppose
that perfect obedience to spiritual law would
result in physical immortality.

The death that is the consequence of disobedience to spiritual law must be spiritual death.
The *soul* that sinneth, *it* shall die.

As by loving God the spiritual nature is

nourished, so by refusing to love him it famishes. As the branch must wither when it is severed from the vine, so the soul must decay when it is cut off from the source of its life. As darkness follows when light is withdrawn, so spiritual death must supervene when spiritual life ceases. It is not a judicial infliction: it is a natural result.

But what are the symptoms by which the presence of spiritual death is known? In physical death there is not a cessation of activity, but a change of activity. In the dead body the forces of nature are at work, not less industriously than in the living body, but their products in the two cases are altogether dissimilar. In the one case they are compacting and strengthening the frame: in the other case they are destroying it. Life builds up: death pulls down what life has built.

The same thing is true of the spiritual nature. While the soul lives by obedience to its law, all its powers work together harmoniously, building up a perfect character. There is no schism in the soul. The faculties that ought to rule, rule. The faculties that ought to serve, serve. The soul is growing daily in grace and manliness and vigor. But when the law is disobeyed, and death ensues, a process very like that of the dissolution of the body begins.

There is discord and confusion among the faculties. The malignant passions and the selfish desires and the animal cravings usurp the places that belong to reason and conscience and the pure affections. The nature is completely inverted. The powers that ought to rule are made to serve; and those that ought to serve are allowed to rule. The whole nature is thus thrown into disorder. The process going on within is demolition.

But what is this spiritual nature of which we are speaking? I include under the term, the nobler faculties of the soul; its natural love of truth and beauty and goodness; its instinctive reverence and trust and generous affection; its native courage and honor and magnanimity. All men do, by nature, possess such qualities as these; and it is because they possess these qualities, that they are said to be made in the image of God. This is that part of the human nature by which we are brought into communion with the divine being. This is that part of the human nature which is enlarged and invigorated by obedience of the soul's law, — by loving God and men.

But by disobedience of the soul's law, these faculties are injured and finally destroyed. Every act of sin helps to dull the moral sense, to impair the moral judgment, to dethrone the

reason, and to paralyze the nobler affections.
Every violation of the law of love to God and
man inflicts upon this part of the nature a grave
injury. Every lie that a man tells weakens his
love of the truth, and makes the next lie easier.
Every act of cruelty hardens his heart, and ren-
ders him less sensitive to the sufferings of others.
Every outbreak of anger makes it harder for
him to restrain his resentments. Every act and
every harbored thought of impurity taints the
very fountains of his life. Every deed of dis-
honesty helps to fix him in the habit of dishon-
esty. All sin is thus seen to propagate itself.
Evil deeds are evil seeds that spring up before
many days, and bear fruit in the life, some
thirty, some sixty, some an hundred fold. The
result of sin is not only suffering, but also sin.
" Whatsoever a man soweth, *that* shall he also
reap." He who sows sin reaps *sin.* The seed
springs up quickly, grows rapidly, multiplies at
a fearful rate, and brings forth in the life a rank
and terrible harvest.

Such a process of moral deterioration always
goes on in the life of him who habitually dis-
obeys the law of God. When it has gone on
long enough, the moral sense will be completely
gone ; the love of truth and goodness and
beauty will be supplanted by selfishness and
malignity ; reverence will give place to scepti-

cism, affection to cynical contempt. When this process once begins, it will go on without interruption to the bitter and dreadful end, unless some supernatural and new creative agency come in to arrest it. This is not a remedial, but a destructive process. It is spiritual decay, ending in death. The soul that sinneth, it shall not be purified by sinning: it shall die. The soul is disobeying its organic law; and for every existence, whether spiritual or physical, the penalty of disobedience to its organic law is death.

Of course the moral deterioration which comes upon the soul as the natural consequence of disobedience is not unaccompanied by suffering. In its earlier stages, at least, this decay is not painless. To have known the right, and yet to have refused to do it; to have lost the consciousness of integrity, and gained the consciousness of degradation and helplessness, — all this fills the soul at times with unutterable distress. " The *way* of the transgressor is hard," whatever his end may be.

The penalty of God's law is not, as some people coarsely conceive, mere physical pain or temporal calamity. Some persons who believe that sin is punished in this life point, for proof of their theory, to the afflictions and losses that evil-doers suffer. But these providential sufferings are not, as any one can see, distributed by any rule of merit. Many bad men prosper outwardly; many good men are overwhelmed with disasters. No one has a right to say that the misfortunes that overtake a man are the penalties of his evil-doing. The real penalty of sin is not temporal distress: it is spiritual death. As sin is in its essence a spiritual fact, so the punishment of sin must be in its essence a spiritual fact. The death that is the consequence of sin is the decay and final ruin of the spiritual nature.

We have noted now the effect upon the individual, of disobedience to the perfect law; but another element enters into the problem. As obedience to the first commandment of the law, that bids us love God with all the heart, would result in building up in the soul a perfect character, so obedience to the second command, that bids us love our neighbors as ourselves, would result in building up in the world a perfect society.

As disobedience to the first command of Christ produces in the soul mutiny and conflict among its faculties, so disobedience to the second command results in strife and disorder among men. "Thou shalt love thy neighbor as thyself," is the organic law of a perfect society. Where that law is disobeyed there is confusion and every evil work; and therefore every individual sinner must suffer not only the misery resulting from his own distempers and corruptions, but also that which accrues to him as being an integral part of a fallen society.

It will not be denied that the law which requires us to love God with all the heart, and our neighbors as ourselves, is, and by the great majority of men always has been, habitually disobeyed. And we are often told that the penalty of this law cannot be remitted without weakening the government of God; that God has said, "The soul that sinneth, it shall die," and that God must not break his word; that therefore by and by, after death and in eternity, the penalty of the law will be executed upon all transgressors who have not accepted of Christ as their substitute. Is this true? No, it is not true, because it is not half the truth. It is not true, that by and by after death, in eternity, the penalty of the law will begin to be executed upon impenitent transgressors. The penalty of the law begins to be executed upon every transgressor at the very moment of his sin. "To be carnally-minded *is* death," — not will be death by and by. That death which is the penalty of the law; that death which is the portion of all that are carnally minded; which reveals itself in the degradation of the individual, in his gradual loss of moral principle, in the weakening of those instincts within him that approve whatever things are pure and lovely and of good report, in the growth of his selfish desires and his animal cravings and his malignant passions, and in the torments with which they fill his soul; the death that also exhibits itself in the mischiefs that abound in society, in the envyings and jealousies, the strifes and the wars, the robberies and the debaucheries, the bitterness and woe under which the whole creation groaneth and travaileth together, — this tremendous fact of spiritual death is not, alas! any thing to be waited for. It is here; it is all about us: we have felt its ravages in our own souls; we have seen the corruption and devastation with which it is filling society. The retributions of God's law are falling on every side, thicker and more deadly than the iron storm that beats against the battlements at Kars, or ploughs the banks of the beautiful blue Danube.

The court of God is not adjourned until some unknown future day: he sitteth now upon the circle of the heavens; the unchangeable laws of the human soul are his swift ministers and executioners, and the penalties of his law begin to be visited upon every sinner at the moment of his transgression. They were never on behalf of any man remitted, and they never will be. What worse hell does any righteous soul crave than that which sin makes in the heart of every sinner, and in the society where iniquity is free to do its deadly work? And when it is seen that this woe and degradation must, in the nature of things, go on propagating themselves by their own law of increase, does any one need to fear that God's law will be dishonored through any laxity of administration?

When the fact is once comprehended, that God's law is spiritual, that its penalty is spiritual death, and that the relation between sin and its penalty is the relation of cause and effect, many things become plain. It begins to be clear, for one thing, that all talk about transferring penalty or substituting something else for penalty is nonsense. Nothing can be substituted for the curse that falls upon the soul of a man who tells a lie.

The fact of retribution we have now fully considered, as it affects the character of the individual and the condition of society. Let us now note a little more narrowly the effect of the operation of this law upon the *feelings* of the individual. How does this process through which the soul passes after disobedience report itself in consciousness?

Of course there is, to begin with, a sense of ill-desert and a feeling of shame. The man who

does a wrong act is degraded in his own eyes.
The man who lives a life of disobedience to
God's law feels guilty.

There is also a feeling that punishment is
deserved, and a vague dread of coming retribution. What is the meaning of this feeling?
Punishment is inflicted, as we have seen ; why,
then, is it dreaded? The answer is, that the
dread is simply the reverberation in man's consciousness of that note of doom which is all
the while sounding through God's universe as a
warning to every evil-doer. The conscience
which says, " I ought *now* to do right," does not
say, " I ought by and by to suffer because I
have done wrong : " it says, "I ought to suffer
now, and doubtless I shall continue to suffer,
because the thing that is wrong will be wrong
for ever and ever." The moral sense does not
bear witness to any different kind of punishment beyond the veil, from that which we here
endure because of sin : it only bears witness
that this will continue and probably increase in
the future ; that the bad mind will make for itself a bad element, and dwell in misery on the
other side of the grave as surely as on this side.
Faith and obedience give us the *substance* of the
things we hope for, — the substance of heaven.
Unbelief and disobedience give us the substance
of the things we dread, — the substance of hell.

Nevertheless the good man hopes for much that he does not see, and the evil man dreads a future that he knows is full of increasing woe.

But there is still another feeling, most central and troublesome of all, that takes up its abode in the heart of the transgressor, and will not be driven forth. That is the feeling that God is angry with him. In the place of that glad confidence with which the soul ought to approach the heavenly Father, there is cold suspicion and alienation. We are always inclined to hate and suspect, not only those who have wronged us, but especially those whom we have wronged. It is almost impossible for us to believe that one whom we have deeply injured does not cherish resentment toward us. And this is precisely the feeling which the sinner finds in his heart whenever he thinks of God. By this instinct of his nature he is driven farther and farther away from God; his sins have separated betwixt him and God; and every act of disobedience increases the distance that divides him from the Being in whose presence alone there is life and peace.

Such is the condition of every man who has transgressed the law of God. His sin has degraded him, crippled his best faculties, dulled his moral sense, and weakened his will. His sin has made him ashamed of himself, and afraid of

God. What now can Christ the Son of God do for this unhappy man? If he is ever to be rescued from the bottomless pit into which he is sinking, the divine power must rescue him. That is the work that the Saviour came into this world to do. His name is called Jesus, because he saves his people from their sins. But how does he save them? What does he do for them?

To begin with, it is clear, I think, that what he does is done directly for and upon them, rather than upon God and his government.

He does not change God's feelings toward us, because God has always loved us. To say that the effect of the work of the Son is to change the feelings of the Father, is to make of the Son and the Father two distinct beings. If they are really one, as we profess to believe, then what one thinks and feels the other thinks and feels. If the feelings of the Father are changed by the act of the Son, then there are either two gods, or the Son is not God.

He does not suffer the penalty of our sins in our stead. That would be unjust and immoral if it were possible; and our study of the nature of law and penalty has shown that it is impossible.

He does not " substitute his own voluntary sacrificial chastisement " for the penalty due to us. The penalty of sin is spiritual death, moral corruption, and ruin. Nothing can be substituted for this penalty. With every sin the penalty is inseparably connected ; and it is no more possible to substitute something else for that penalty than it would be to step in after the flash of the lightning, and substitute some other noise — the report of a pistol, say — for the peal of thunder.

No : it is not necessary that God's wrath should be appeased, nor that God's law should be saved from dishonor. There was no obstacle in the heart of God nor in the government of God in the way of the restoration of transgressors. The only obstacle was in the sinner's own corrupted heart and weakened will.

What, then, does Christ do for us?

1. He reconciles us to God, not God to us. " God was in Christ, reconciling the world unto himself." The first need of every transgressor is to be made to feel that, in spite of the wrong that he has done to his Father, his Father loves him, and will pardon and save him if he will but repent and return. It is hard, as we have seen, to inspire this confidence in the sinner. Even here and now, with the gospel in our hands, and the story of Calvary a household word, men will hardly believe that God is willing to forgive them. How much less possible

would it have been if that marvellous revelation of God's love had never been made!

To this world of sinful men, lost and helpless in their degradation, fleeing in dread from the presence of God, Christ comes. His hands are full of blessings; miracles of help and healing crowd the brief hours of his ministry; though sharp rebukes of hypocrisy and meanness are sometimes heard from his lips, yet to the multitudes his voice is a voice of tenderness and grace; he is one who goes about doing good, and speaking as never man spake; and he says of himself continually, that he is not only Son of man, but Son of God, — nay, that he and the Father are one. By this divine life, by these transcendent personal claims, he arouses the enmity of the Jewish hierarchy. Their craft is in danger. The doctrine of this Teacher will overthrow their cumbersome ritual machinery, and substitute for it a simpler faith. Therefore at their hands he suffers constant persecution until at length, bursting forth with fiendish rage, they cry out, "Crucify him!" and lead him forth to prison and to death.

It was done in Judæa nineteen centuries ago, but the bad passions that begot the bad deed live in the human nature in every age. No man can deny that *his* sins crucified the Saviour, unless he can deny that the human nature belongs to him ; unless he is sure that he never had an unkind feeling toward a rival, and that he never felt cross or resentful toward another whose good conduct shamed or reproved him.

The Saviour knew when he came that suffering and death would surely be his portion. He knew that the selfishness and the malice of men would not suffer him to live on the earth, that if he did bear witness to the truth they would slay him ; he knew that his life of unwearied love would end upon the cross. Yet he shrunk not from this fiery baptism ; for he knew also that when men had glutted their rage upon him, when they stood beneath his cross, and looked on him whom they had pierced, when they remembered his deeds of mercy and his words of gentle pleading, — how he had borne their griefs and carried their sorrows all his life, — that a great horror of remorse and contrition would fill their souls, and that they would smite upon their breasts, saying, " Truly this was a righteous man !" And when the third day after, the bars of his sepulchre were broken, and he came forth leading captivity captive, and proving his divinity by this last and most infallible proof, then he knew that there would be a mighty reaction in the hearts of men towards him, and that in remembering the life and the death of Him who claimed to be one with God, they could no longer have any doubt that God loved them. Such a demonstration as this of what God is willing to do that men may be saved would, he knew, conquer their enmity and their suspicion, and bring them in penitence and trust to his feet.

That, at any rate, is the fact of history. Christ said, " And I, if I be lifted up from the earth, will draw all men unto me." The prophecy has been abundantly fulfilled. In all the ages, men looking on the cross of Christ have seen in it a proof of God's love for them ; and, believing in his love, have come to him, confessing their sins, and consecrating their lives to the service of Him who died for them.

They are sinners still, and sinners they must always be. They can never remember without regret their past evil doings ; but the fact that sweeps away all this bad consciousness of guilt and dread is the fact that is brought home to them with such mighty power in the cross of Christ, — that God loves them with an infinite love. Unworthy they are ; but they have no right to despise themselves, or to despair of themselves, after he has shown such love for them.

Thus it was, in the language of Paul, that " when we were enemies we were reconciled to God by the death of his Son." Thus it was that we who "sometime were afar off were made nigh by the blood of Christ."

2. But this is only the beginning of what he does for us. "If when we were enemies we were reconciled to God by the death of his Son, *much more*, being reconciled, we shall be saved by his life." Being brought back to God in loving confidence, being re-united with him by faith, we again become partakers of the divine nature. To the law of God we are again, in our ruling choice, obedient; and the result of obedience to that law is spiritual life. "You hath he quickened" (or restored to life), says Paul, "who were dead in trespasses and sins." The branch that was separated from the vine, and that was withering and dying, is again grafted upon the parent stock, and life returns to it. So long as that vital union continues, the soul will live.

Thus although spiritual death is the consequence of sin, and though there is not in nature nor within the power of man any deliverance from this death, yet in Christ who is our life, we are raised from the dead. By receiving of the infinite fulness of his divine life, spiritual life is renewed in us. Sitting at his feet, and learning of him, we receive his spirit; a remedial and restorative work begins; our habits of thought and of feeling are changed; until at length death no longer reigns in our natures, for we are alive unto God through Jesus Christ our Lord.

Through man's disobedience the order of nature has become to him the minister of wrath and ruin ; if he is ever to be saved from the destruction which he has thus invoked upon himself, it must be by the intervention of a power above nature. The natural order must not be set aside, but a remedial order may be instituted whose function it shall be to repair the ruin sin has wrought. For the poison of sin, the effect of which must be death, the supernatural grace of God in Christ is the antidote. The curse is in the nature of things ; the cure is from above nature. What the law could not do, God has done by sending his Son. Love can do many things that law cannot do ; nevertheless the two agencies work together as co-ordinate forces in Christ's kingdom. The grace does not make void the law : the law does not prevent the grace. I do not set aside the law of gravitation if I pick up and place upon his feet a lame man who has fallen, and cannot rise. Perhaps he cannot even stand and walk after he is lifted up, without being held up and steadied ; and yet it may be necessary to his recovery that he should stand and walk. If I put my arm about him, then, and walk with him, I do not set aside the law of gravitation : I simply counteract the effects of its working upon him. The law of gravitation is a good law ; yet, through his own fault or infirmity, it may become the instrument of injury to my neighbor. Then I have a right to interfere by my will to counteract its injurious effects. Is the law of gravitation dishonored when its injurious effects are thus mercifully overruled? Does the lame man respect that law any less because I hold him up when he is too feeble to stand ?

A benevolent will may thus, without casting any discredit upon law or interfering with the uniformity of its operations, modify the processes of nature, and prevent the results that her laws are producing. Man can do this: is it not likely that God can do more? Without weakening the force of any of his moral or spiritual laws, he can bring into this scene of disorder and ruin, a grace that is mightier to save than the forces already at work are to destroy.,

Humanity, lying crippled and helpless outside the beautiful gate of the temple of the Holy, hears Christ saying, " Rise up and walk," and, grasping the almighty hand that is extended, is lifted up from degradation and infirmity. The outstretched hand may be refused ; that power is granted to human wills : if it be refused, there is no other power that can save. But he who will accept its aid, disabled though he may be by his own sin, shall be lifted up; "yea, he shall be holden up, for God is able to make him stand."

This, then, is the substance of the work that Jesus Christ comes into the world to do. To conquer the enmity and suspicion of men by his own great sacrifice; to make them believe that God loves them; then, having won their confidence, to repair, by the communication of his own life-giving spirit, the ruin that sin has wrought in their natures; to restore their souls that are sinking in spiritual death, to life and health and peace, — this is what Christ does for men. He reconciles us by his death: he saves us by his life.

It will be objected to this explanation of the work of Christ, that it does not accord with the Scripture. The sufferings of Christ, it will be said, are there spoken of as judicially laid upon him. The penalties of sin are in the Bible represented as positive inflictions from the hand of a judge, not as results taking place in the order of nature. That is true; and the difficulty cannot be fully explained without entering upon a more elaborate discussion of the principles which ought to govern Biblical interpretation, than there is room for in this place. Of that more, perhaps, hereafter. It is sufficient to say that the Bible does not always state the truths of religion with scientific precision ; that many of those texts which are made the subjects of grammatical and logical analysis are simply the expression of deep religious feeling. Such expressions will always take a highly objective and poetical form. If, therefore, we find texts which represent Christ as suffering judicially in our stead, and God as being propitiated by his sufferings, we need not deny the first principles of morality. It is possible, surely, that these words may be figures ; but it is not possible that penalty should be transferred from a guilty being to an innocent one, nor that the wrath of God against a sinner should be appeased by the suffering of one sinless person, nor that any thing whatever should be substituted for that spiritual death which is the inevitable penalty of violated spiritual law.

The conception of a reign of law had not been reached by the people to whom the Scripture was first given, and the truth was put in language that they could understand. Much that we know takes place under laws of the strictest uniformity is represented in the Bible as the direct effect of God's volition. It is not true that the natural order is any less divine than the supernatural interposition,

" For if He thunder by law, the thunder is still His voice : "

but when it becomes plain to us that the retributions of the moral law are part of the uniform course of nature, we are delivered from
a great deal of needless anxiety about the foun-
dations of God's moral government.

www.ingramcontent.com/pod-product-compliance
Lightning Source LLC
Chambersburg PA
CBHW021525090426
42739CB00007B/788